NATURE'S FURY

VOLCANO!

Anita Ganeri

ARCTURUS

This edition first published by Arcturus Publishing
Distributed by Black Rabbit Books
123 South Broad Street
Mankato
Minnesota MN 56001

Copyright © 2006 Arcturus Publishing

Printed in China

Library of Congress Cataloging-in-Publication Data
Ganeri, Anita 1961-
    Volcano! / by Anita Ganeri
        p. cm. -- (Nature's fury)
Includes index
ISBN-13: 978-1-84193-561-4 (alk. paper)
1. Volcanoes--Juvenile literature. 2. Natural disasters--Juvenile literature.
I. Title

QE521.3.G366 2007
363.34'95--dc22

                          2006022608

9 8 7 6 5 4 3 2

Editor: Alex Woolf
Design: Mind's Eye Design
Picture Research: Shelley Noronha

Picture credits:
Corbis: 23 (Roger Ressmeyer), 27 (Reuters)

Frank Lane Picture Agency: 10.

NASA: 18 (Jeff Schmaltz, MODIS Rapid Response Team, NASA/GSFC),
20 (Landsat 7 project and EROS Data Center), 21 (Jacques Descloitres, MODIS Rapid
Response Team, NASA/GSFC)

Rex Features: 9 (The Travel Library), 12 (Sipa Press), 13 (Sipa Press), 14 (Rich/Wasaki),
22 (Eye Ubiquitous), 25 (Mauro Carraro), 26 (Mauro Carraro)

Science Photo Library: 4 (Krafft/Explorer), 5 (G. Brad Lewis), 6 (Simon Fraser),
7 (Gary Hincks), 8 (Gary Hincks), 11 (Ray Fairbanks), 15 (Bernhard Edmaier),
16 (Dennis Flaherty), 17 (Tony Craddock), 19 (Stephen and Donna O'Meara),
24 (Krafft/Hoa-Qui), 28 (Adam G. Sylvester), 29 (Anne Kahle, JPL-Caltech)

Contents

What Are Volcanoes?

▼ *A spectacular fountain of lava shooting from a volcano on the island of Bali in Indonesia.*

A volcano is a hill or mountain where molten rock spurts to the surface from deep underground. Aboveground, the magma is known as lava. A volcano is made up of lava that has cooled and solidified, together with cinders and ash. Volcanic eruptions are among the most violent and spectacular natural events on earth. Accompanied by red-hot rivers of lava, towering clouds of ash, and thick flows of mud, they can devastate the landscape and people's lives.

Volcanoes have been erupting since the earth was formed 4.5 billion years ago. Today, about 25 volcanoes around the world erupt every year on land. Some of these active volcanoes erupt almost all the time. Others may erupt only once every few hundred years. Some volcanoes erupt with giant explosions. Others erupt more gently, producing fizzing lava fountains.

Volcanoes and the landscape

Much of earth's surface is made up of rocks that have come from volcanoes. Volcanoes create and build mountains and islands, but they can also be also destructive. They cover the landscape with lava, ash, and mud, burning and burying plants and destroying animal habitats. Houses, villages, and towns may also be buried or burned. In the past, eruptions have killed thousands of people.

Vulcan's island

The word *volcano* comes from "Vulcano", the name of an island off the coast of Italy. The ancient Romans believed that the god Vulcan lived in a volcano on the island, where he made weapons for the other gods, such as arrows, armor and lightning bolts. Fiery eruptions from the island's volcanoes were believed to be sparks from Vulcan's forge.

◄ *Molten lava cools to form new rock. This school bus was caught in a lava flow in Hawaii and is now trapped in rock forever.*

CASE STUDY

Krakatau

One of the biggest volcanic eruptions ever recorded happened in 1883. A volcano on the tiny island of Krakatau in Indonesia erupted with a series of enormous explosions. The explosions were so loud they could be heard more than 3,000 miles (5,000 kilometers) away. The island itself was blasted to pieces, leaving a massive crater 957 feet (290 meters) deep. But the effects of the eruption were felt far and wide. Hot ash clouds destroyed villages 30 miles (50 kilometers) away across the sea, and giant waves swamped nearby coasts, killing 36,000 people. A new volcano called Anak Krakatau (child of Krakatau) is growing where Krakatau erupted.

How Do Volcanoes Form?

▼ *Iceland is on a boundary between two tectonic plates that are moving away from each other. The rocks here are being torn apart, making giant cracks in the landscape.*

Volcanoes form in places where molten rock forces its way upward through a crack in the earth's surface. The molten rock, or magma, comes from many miles underground, from a layer of the earth called the mantle. The mantle lies beneath the solid upper layer of the earth, called the crust. On the continents, the crust is about 30 miles (50 kilometers) thick, while under the oceans, it is about 3 miles (5 kilometers) thick.

Moving plates

The crust is cracked into huge pieces called tectonic plates. The plates drift on the hot rock beneath, but they move only an inch or so a year. Scientists think they are moved by slow, swirling currents in the mantle. Most volcanoes form where two plates meet. The lines between plates are called plate boundaries.

At some boundaries, two plates collide, and one plate dives under the other and into the mantle. These boundaries are called destructive boundaries or subduction zones. The plate that dives down melts, making magma that rises again to produce volcanoes. At other boundaries, two plates move apart. These are called constructive boundaries. Magma rises up from the mantle to fill the gap between the plates.

Submerged volcanoes

Many more volcanoes are hidden under the oceans than can be seen on land. Most form along constructive boundaries on the ocean floor, where magma leaks out between tectonic plates that are moving apart. These boundaries are also called spreading ridges. The magma solidifies to make new crust on each side of the boundary. Other undersea volcanoes form at hot spots (*see box*) and at destructive boundaries.

◄ *Oahu, one of the Hawaiian Islands, is the tip of a hot-spot volcano. The volcano is fed by magma that leaks through the crust from below.*

HOT-SPOT VOLCANOES

Some volcanoes grow in the middle of tectonic plates, far from where plates are colliding or spreading apart. Scientists think that they form over "hot spots" in the mantle, where magma forces it way up through the crust. Hot-spot volcanoes in the middle of oceans form undersea mountains called seamounts. The islands of Hawaii in the middle of the Pacific Ocean are the summits of giant seamounts.

Inside a Volcano

At the top of a volcano, there is often a dish-shaped hollow called a crater. Beneath the crater is a hole called a vent that stretches down into the earth's crust. At the bottom of the vent, is a chamber full of magma, which may be 60 miles (100 kilometers) or more underground. During an eruption, magma rises from the magma chamber, through the vent, and out into the air.

A composite cone

Most volcanoes on land, such as Mount Fuji in Japan and Vesuvius in Italy, are tall cones made up of layers of broken lava and ash. The layers were formed by many eruptions over hundreds, thousands or millions of years. A main vent in the center and side vents lead to the volcano's lower slopes. This type of volcano is called a composite cone or stratovolcano. It is like a giant heap of loose rubble. Magma sometimes flows in between the layers of lava and ash and then solidifies, making the volcano more stable.

▲ *A composite cone or stratovolcano. Magma rises up the vent from the magma chamber. The volcano's layers consist of material from previous eruptions.*

Magma ingredients

Magma is molten rock underground (molten rock on the surface is called lava). Some types of magma are runny and flow easily, like syrup. Others are thick and sticky, like tar. Magma has a temperature of about a thousand degrees.

Magma also contains gas dissolved in it. When magma is deep inside the earth, high pressure keeps the gas dissolved. But when the magma rises through the vent of a volcano, the gas is released and bursts out of the volcano with the molten rock. This is exactly what happens when you open a fizzy drink. Gas dissolved in the liquid bubbles out when you open the can or bottle, releasing the pressure.

ACTIVE, DORMANT, AND EXTINCT

Scientists classify volcanoes as active, dormant, or extinct. An active volcano is a volcano that people have seen erupt in the past few thousand years. There are about 500 active volcanoes in the world. A dormant volcano is an active volcano that is not erupting at the moment. An extinct volcano is a volcano that nobody has ever seen erupt and is not expected to erupt again—although that doesn't mean it never will!

▲ *Sugarloaf Mountain in Rio de Janeiro, Brazil, is made of magma that solidified in the vent of a volcano. The volcano's cone has been eroded away over thousands of years.*

Shields and Cinders

Not all volcanic eruptions are the same. Gentle eruptions produce rivers of red-hot lava. Violent eruptions produce towering clouds of ash but very little lava. Other eruptions produce both ash and lava. These different types of eruption build different types of volcano.

▼ *Fountains of lava form where runny lava reaches the surface and is blown into the air by gases.*

Shield volcanoes

Shield volcanoes are made by gentle eruptions. They happen at constructive boundaries and at hot spots, where thin, runny lava comes up from the ground.

A shield volcano is wide and low with gently sloping sides, like an upside-down plate. During an eruption, gas in the magma makes it shoot upward, firing blobs of lava out of the vent in spectacular fountains. The lava falls to the ground and flows down the volcano's sides in glowing rivers called lava flows. Gradually, the lava cools and turns to solid rock. Over thousands or millions of years, the lava flows build on top of each other to make a mountain.

Powerful eruptions can throw blobs of lava hundreds of feet into the air. Large blobs, called bombs, weigh several tons. Two types of lava are produced, called pahoehoe and aa. Pahoehoe cools to form round heaps with a surface like coiled rope. When aa cools, it forms jagged lumps. *Pahoehoe* and *aa* are Hawaiian words.

Cinder cones

Sometimes the gas in magma forms bubbles in the blobs of lava that hurtle out of a volcano. The blobs cool in the air and fall to the ground as red or black pieces of rock called cinders. The cinders pile up to form a steep-sided volcano called a cinder cone. Cinder cones often form on the sides of shield volcanoes.

HAWAIIAN ERUPTIONS

Eruptions that produce lava fountains and lava flows are called Hawaiian eruptions because they happen regularly on the island of Hawaii in the Pacific Ocean. Hawaii is made up of five giant shield volcanoes. One of them, called Kilauea, is the most active volcano on earth. It has been erupting almost constantly since 1983, producing fountains of red and yellow lava thousands of feet high.

▲ *Cinder cones on the island of Maui in the Hawaiian Islands. Cinder cones often form in groups.*

Explosive Volcanoes

▲ *The volcano on the Caribbean island of Montserrat erupted violently in 1997. Much of the island was buried under ash.*

Volcanoes at destructive boundaries erupt violently. The eruptions are dramatic and dangerous and have created the greatest explosions in earth's history. These eruptions happen because the magma at destructive boundaries is thick and sticky. It blocks a volcano's vent until the pressure from the magma chamber underneath builds up so much that the magma is forced upward.

Plinian eruptions

The gas in the magma cannot bubble upward because the magma is too thick. Instead, it explodes, blasting the molten rock into tiny pieces. These violent eruptions build steep-sided volcanoes made up of layers of ash and lava called composite cones or stratovolcanoes (*see page 8*). The eruptions are known as Plinian eruptions after Pliny the Elder, a Roman who died in the explosive eruption of Mount Vesuvius in 79 CE.

During a Plinian eruption, a high-speed jet of hot gas fires tiny pieces of molten rock into the air. These pieces are smaller than grains of sand but quickly solidify to form clouds of ash. The gas jet eventually slows down, but the hot gases continue to float upward through the atmosphere, carrying the ash with them. The towering cloud of ash is called an eruption column. The biggest eruptions produce columns more than 30 miles (50 kilometers) high.

Volcanic hurricanes

Ash clouds are often so thick with ash and small drops of molten rock that they cannot keep rising into the air. Instead, they collapse and surge down the sides of a volcano. These billowing avalanches of red-hot ash and gas are called pyroclastic flows or volcanic hurricanes. They travel at speeds up to 96 miles (160 kilometers) per hour.

CASE STUDY

Mount Pinatubo

The eruption of Mount Pinatubo in the Philippines in 1991 was one of the most violent eruptions ever witnessed. Pinatubo had not erupted for 400 years. The eruption began with rumbling noises from the mountain. It ended with a series of massive explosions that blew 660 feet (200 meters) off the top of the mountain and formed an ash cloud 24 miles (40 kilometers) high, turning the sky black for weeks. The cloud spread all around the world. Pyroclastic flows spread more than nine miles (15 kilometers) from the volcano.

▲ *A pyroclastic flow pours down the slopes of Mount Unzen in Japan during the eruption of 1991. Forty journalists were killed as they tried to photograph these flows.*

Mountains and Islands

Ash, lava, and cinders that have spewed out from volcanoes build up the landscape. Volcanoes start life as vents in the ground. As soon as they start erupting, a hill begins to form from the ash, lava, or cinders. Eventually the hill may become a volcano several miles high.

▼ *The perfect cone of Mount Fuji in Japan rises to 12,460 feet (3,776 meters). Mount Fuji last erupted in 1707.*

Shield volcanoes are made from layers of lava that flow down their sides. Cinder cones are heaps of loose cinders. Composite volcanoes are heaps of ash and lava built up in layers. Volcanoes can be single mountains, such as Mount Fuji in Japan, or part of huge mountain ranges, such as the Andes in South America.

Volcanic islands

Lava that erupts on the seafloor piles up into undersea mountains called sea mounts. If the volcano continues to erupt, it eventually breaks the surface and forms a new island. Volcanic islands grow along destructive boundaries. They form long, curving chains of islands called island arcs.

Volcanic islands also form over hot spots and sometimes over spreading ridges. The island of Hawaii is the tip of a sea mount that rises 29,700 feet (9,000 meters) from the seabed, making it the tallest mountain on earth.

Igneous rocks

When volcanic rock cools and solidifies, it forms igneous, or fiery, rock. There are many different types of igneous rocks. For example, runny lava from shield volcanoes cools to make a black rock called basalt. The part of the earth's crust that forms the seabed is made from basalt. It forms when lava flows out at spreading ridges. Volcanic ash that falls from clouds and pyroclastic flows builds up in thick layers. Gradually, the bottom layers are squeezed together and turn into a rock called tuff.

▲ *A volcanic island off the north coast of Iceland. It is covered with craters that formed as hot gases bubbled up through the cooling lava.*

CASE STUDY

A volcano grows

In February 1943, a Mexican farmer named Dionisio Pulido began to feel small earthquakes and noticed that the ground under his feet was warm. Soon a crack opened in his fields, and ash and lava began to pour out. A volcano began erupting in front of his eyes! By July, the volcano was 990 feet (300 meters) high and Dionisio's village had been buried. The eruption eventually stopped in 1952.

Volcano Destruction

▲ *A gaping hole is left where the summit of Mount St. Helens, once stood. The mountain was blown apart in 1980 by a gigantic volcanic explosion.*

Volcanic eruptions build up volcanoes and make new rock, but the eruptions of composite cone volcanoes are also very destructive. They blow volcanoes to pieces and create vast holes in the earth's surface.

Blowing its top

The eruption of a large volcano can be so violent that it blows the top off the volcano, leaving the volcano hundreds of feet lower than before. This happens when thick magma has built up inside the vent but cannot get out. Ash and rock are blown into the air and also cascade down the mountainside.

Composite volcanoes cannot keep growing upward forever. Eventually, they become unstable. Then pressure from the magma inside makes their upper slopes bulge and collapse, sending down massive avalanches of ash and rock that spread for many miles. This also releases the magma, which explodes sideways out of the volcano.

Calderas

A caldera is a giant volcanic crater. A caldera forms when explosive eruptions leave an empty space in a volcano's magma chamber, and the ground above collapses into the chamber. Small calderas are a few miles across. The largest ones found are more than 30 miles (50 kilometers) across and were formed by gigantic eruptions in the distant past.

Three of the largest calderas on earth are in Yellowstone National Park. The widest is 36 miles (60 kilometers) across. They were formed by the eruption and collapse of incredibly large volcanoes more than 500,000 years ago. Several miles under Yellowstone, the magma from the eruptions is still hot. The heat creates the hot springs and geysers that tourists flock to the park to see. The Yellowstone eruptions were a thousand times more powerful than the eruption of Mount St. Helens (*see box*) and buried half of North America under ash.

◄ *Crater Lake in Oregon lies in a caldera formed when Mount Mazama collapsed in a volcanic eruption 7,700 years ago. The cone-shaped island in the center is a sign that volcanic activity is continuing.*

CASE STUDY

Mount St. Helens

The top of Mount St. Helens in Washington State was blown apart by an eruption in 1980. The eruption began with small earthquakes caused by magma moving underground. Ash clouds rose from the crater. Then the north face of the mountain began to bulge outward. Eventually, the bulge collapsed and slid downwards in a massive avalanche. The collapse released magma that exploded, blowing 1,320 feet (400 meters) of the mountaintop to pieces and leaving a gaping hole.

Environmental Effects

▼ *A satellite photograph shows a plume of ash blowing away from Mount Etna on the island of Sicily in Italy. Winds can carry ash hundreds of miles.*

The lava, ash, and gas from a volcanic eruption can affect the countryside all around the volcano. Lava flows spread across the landscape, covering it and burning and burying trees and fields. Most lava flows are slow moving and travel only a couple of miles before they cool and stop. But ash clouds and pyroclastic flows from violent eruptions are much more dangerous.

Ash layers

Violent eruptions from volcanoes throw vast clouds of ash into the atmosphere. Scientists estimate that in 1980, a staggering 1.7 cubic miles (2.5 cubic kilometers) of ash erupted from Mount St. Helens. That is enough ash to fill 5,000 Olympic stadiums. Winds can carry the clouds, leaving a dusting of ash on the ground hundreds of miles from the eruption. Deep ash deposits make it impossible for plants to grow, turning green countryside into a gray desert.

Pyroclastic flows have the most devastating effects. They sweep downhill, scorching the ground with hot gas, ash, and rocks as they go. Trees are knocked down and burned, and animals are killed instantly.

Global effects

Ash from the biggest eruptions travels more than nine miles (15 kilometers) up into the atmosphere. It stays there for weeks or months and is carried by winds for thousands of miles—sometimes right around world. This ash blocks sunlight, which can make the weather slightly colder all over the world. Gases from eruptions also cause problems. For example, sulfur dioxide mixes with rain to make acid rain, which slowly kills plants and wildlife in lakes and rivers as it falls.

▲ *The Soufrière Hills volcano on the island of Montserrat in the Caribbean. Pyroclastic flows have stripped the mountainside of vegetation and altered the coastline.*

 CASE STUDY

The year without summer

In 1815, a volcano called Tambora erupted on the Indonesian island of Sumbawa. Scientists think that this was the biggest eruption in the last 10,000 years. It threw 30 times as much ash into the atmosphere as Mount St. Helens in 1980. The ash spread around the world, blocking out the sun. This caused cold, damp weather in many places over many months. Crops didn't grow, causing food shortages that led to riots. In America, 1816 was called "the year without summer."

Mud and Flood

The landscape around volcanoes is not just affected by lava, ash clouds, and pyroclastic flows. Water also causes problems. Water from melting glaciers mixes with ash and pours down the sides of volcanoes in mudflows. Water released in eruptions causes floods, and explosive volcanoes cause giant waves at sea.

Mudflows

Giant composite cone volcanoes are thousands of feet high, and their summits are covered in snow and ice all year round. During an eruption, the heat from the magma melts the snow and ice to make water. The water flows down the volcano's slopes, mixing with ash to form thick mudflows. These flows are called lahars.

▶ *Mount St. Helens, seen from space in 1999. The gray river-like areas are the remains of mudflows that formed from ash and molten snow during the 1980 eruption.*

The mud hurtles along river valleys at speeds of up to 90 miles (150 kilometers) per hour, destroying everything in its path. It can flow up to 180 miles (300 kilometers) before coming to a stop. Then the mud sets hard, like concrete.

Mudflows also happen when heavy rain mixes with fresh falls of ash. The rain often comes from thunderstorms that happen inside ash clouds.

Monster waves

Volcanic eruptions under the sea can cause giant waves called tsunamis. The waves race across the sea at hundreds of miles per hour. In the open sea, tsunamis are only a few yards high. But when they reach coasts, they rear up and water pours inland, devastating coastal areas and causing massive loss of life. Tsunamis are also triggered by underwater earthquakes.

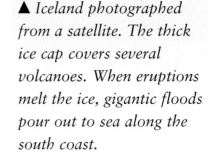

▲ *Iceland photographed from a satellite. The thick ice cap covers several volcanoes. When eruptions melt the ice, gigantic floods pour out to sea along the south coast.*

CASE STUDY

Iceland flood

Part of Iceland is covered in a thick sheet of ice called an ice cap. Underneath the ice cap are several volcanoes. Occasionally, the erupting volcanoes melt the ice, causing floods that flow down to the sea. In 1996, an eruption melted enough water to fill one Olympic-sized swimming pool every second. The water gathered under the ice cap for days before suddenly breaking out in a colossal flood. The flood carried chunks of ice the size of houses for nine miles (15 kilometers) and covered the land between the ice cap and the sea with ash and rock.

Living with Volcanoes

About 500 million people, or one in 10 of the world's population, live in places that are at risk from volcanoes. Their homes could be hit by lava flows, pyroclastic flows or mudflows. Many people live on old lava flows and in valleys that have been swept by mudflows or pyroclastic flows in the past.

Cities at risk

Naples, Italy, could be affected by pyroclastic flows from a major eruption of Vesuvius. Parts of Seattle could be swamped by mudflows if Mount Rainier explodes like Mount St. Helens did. These risks were not known when these cities were founded and as they developed. It would be impossible to move the cities now.

▼ *Plowing fields in the shadow of Mayon, an active volcano in the Philippines. The rich volcanic soil is good for growing crops, but the fields could be swept away by pyroclastic flows.*

Volcanic soil

Millions of people live near volcanoes because there is nowhere else for them to live. Others choose to take a risk because volcanoes produce fertile soil and are good places to farm.

The soil on the lower slopes of volcanoes is made from eroded lava and ash. It is full of minerals that plants need to grow, which makes it excellent for growing crops. Many huge coffee plantations are situated on volcanoes in Central America, for example, and there are many vineyards around Mount Vesuvius. Farmers often return to volcanic slopes even after their farms have been destroyed by eruptions because the soil is so rich.

There are other advantages to living near volcanoes. Volcanic rocks make good building materials. Lava and tuff can be sawn into building blocks, and cinders are used on the surface of paths and roads. The heat from hot rocks in volcanic areas is used to heat water and to generate electricity.

CASE STUDY

Farming on Mayon

The Mayon volcano in the Philippines has a major eruption about every 10 years, sending out ash columns, pyroclastic flows, and mudflows. There is not much farmland in the area, so farmers grow rice, coconut palms, and vegetables on Mayon's slopes. But it is a risky way to live. Tragically, 75 farmers were killed during an eruption in 1993.

▲ *These children live near the Sakurajima volcano in Japan. They always wear helmets on the way to and from school to protect them from rocks hurled out by eruptions.*

Human Disaster

▼ *Many houses on the island of Heimaey, off Iceland, were destroyed by lava flows in 1973.*

Volcanoes can have devastating effects on local communities. They destroy towns and villages, bury farmland, and damage roads, bridges, and electricity supplies.

The greatest volcanic hazards faced by people are pyroclastic flows and mudflows. Lava flows are not usually dangerous because they normally move slowly and people can easily move out of their way. But lava slowly engulfs houses and other buildings, knocking them down and setting them on fire. Farmland covered in lava is useless for many years.

Burning and burying

Pyroclastic flows are much more lethal. They contain hurricane-force, super-hot winds that knock down and burn any buildings in their path. These flows travel so fast that people often cannot outrun them, even in cars.

Mudflows are just as destructive. They sweep buildings away and then form a hard crust around the remains. Ash that settles on buildings looks light and dusty but is as heavy as concrete when the ash is wet, and causes roofs to collapse.

Lava flows, pyroclastic flows, and mudflows also damage the infrastructure of a place by blocking roads and knocking down bridges so that people can no longer get around. They also bring down telephone lines and power lines, making communication difficult. Other damage is harder to see. For example, tiny particles of ash block the air filters of machines. Wet ash damages electrical equipment, and ash clogs sewage plants.

Ash and aircraft

Aircraft are also in danger. If a jet flies into an ash cloud, the ash can damage the engines. In 1982, a Boeing 747 lost power in all four engines when it flew into an ash cloud billowing out from Galunggung volcano in Indonesia at night. The aircraft glided downward for 23,100 feet (7,000 meters) before the crew managed to start up three of the engines and land the plane safely. It was a terrifying ordeal.

CASE STUDY

A deadly mud flow

The volcano of Nevado del Ruiz in Colombia erupted in 1985. It was not a big eruption, but its heat melted ice, which mixed with ash and rushed down a river valley. The resulting mudflow hit the town of Armero, 30 miles (50 kilometers) away, at night, when people were asleep. The town was swept away, and 21,000 people drowned in the mud. Only 2,000 escaped. The remains of Armero are still buried under the dried-out mud.

▲ *Fields and buildings were buried under mudflows that swept through Armero, Colombia, in 1985. Only one in 10 of the town's population survived.*

Rescue and Aid

If scientists think that a major eruption is about to happen, they advise people to evacuate areas that could be hit by lava flows, pyroclastic flows, and mudflows. Sometimes warnings are given too late or never arrive. Even when people are advised to evacuate, they don't always leave. Some don't believe the warnings, and some don't want to leave their homes.

▲ *Rescuers pull a survivor from the ruins of Armero, Colombia, after mudflows from a volcanic eruption destroyed the town.*

To the rescue

When people are caught in an eruption, they need to be rescued. If they have lost their homes, they need immediate shelter and food, and eventually they need help to rebuild their homes or find new ones.

The first job after an eruption is to rescue survivors and search for missing people. Rescue services can then take them to safety outside the eruption zone. Helicopters are especially useful because roads are often blocked or destroyed, making it hard for rescue vehicles to reach survivors. Helicopters can also lift people trapped by mudflows and floods. Emergency services often have problems organizing rescues because communications are damaged.

Cleaning up and moving back

After the rescue operation, the difficult task of cleaning up begins. Where the landscape is covered in lava, or thick layers of ash or mud, it is often impossible for people to return to their old homes, and the area must be abandoned. But thin layers of ash can be swept up and removed. Roads, bridges, and communications have to be rebuilt.

In less economically developed countries, people who lose their land can be left with nothing. Help may be needed from aid agencies to provide people with temporary shelter and food until new homes can be found for them.

CASE STUDY

Aid in Goma

In January 2002, Mount Nyiragongo in the Democratic Republic of Congo erupted suddenly, pouring lava into the streets of the town of Goma. A third of the city was destroyed, and 400,000 people fled to nearby Rwanda. International aid agencies quickly began handing out food and other items such as clothes and blankets. Together with the local authorities, the agencies then established supply depots and distribution points in Goma for people returning to the city. They also set up clean water supplies and sanitation to stop disease from spreading and provided materials for people to rebuild their homes.

▲ *People of Goma carrying their belongings across lava flows in the town's streets. Those who lost their homes were given shelter in camps set up by aid agencies.*

Volcano Science

Scientists who study volcanoes are called vulcanologists. They investigate what happens to volcanoes before they erupt and while they are erupting. These investigations help the scientists to understand how volcanoes work. It also helps them to predict when a volcano could erupt so that people can be evacuated. This is not an easy job because every eruption is different.

▼ A vulcanologist measuring the temperature of lava. He is using a long probe to reach the molten lava. His shiny protective suit reflects some of the intense heat.

Measuring layers

Vulcanologists examine lava flows, layers of ash, mudflows, and volcanic rock around volcanoes. They measure the thickness of different layers of material and how old the layers are. This tells them how often the volcano has erupted in the past and also how violent each eruption was. With this knowledge vulcanologists are able to draw hazard maps showing which areas around the volcano could be hit by future eruptions.

Predicting eruptions

Vulcanologists also make measurements to see if a volcano is about to erupt. The measurements show if magma is beginning to move deep underground. For example, the scientists take samples of gas coming from the volcano's vent. If it contains a gas called sulfur dioxide, then magma is probably rising upward. Measuring devices called seismometers are used to detect earthquakes. Small quakes indicate that magma is on the move.

In 1991, vulcanologists successfully predicted the violent eruption of Mount Pinatubo (*see page 13*). Their seismometers had detected hundreds of small earthquakes, and gas samples had shown an increase in sulfur dioxide. Danger areas around the volcano were evacuated, and the lives of tens of thousands of people were saved.

GROUND MOVEMENTS

The global positioning system (GPS) used for in-car navigation is also used to predict volcanic eruptions. Vulcanologists place GPS receivers on the tops of volcanoes. The receivers detect whether the ground is swelling upward, which indicates that magma is moving up from underneath and an eruption is on the way.

▲ *The island of Stromboli, Italy, seen through a heat-sensing scanner. The different colors show the temperature of the ground. Red areas are recent lava flows giving out heat.*

THE 10 MOST DESTRUCTIVE VOLCANOES

WHEN	WHERE	CASUALTIES
1815	Tambora, Indonesia	92,000
1883	Krakatau, Indonesia	36,500
1902	Mont Pelée, Martinique	29,000
1985	Nevado del Ruiz, Colombia	25,000
1792	Mount Unzen, Japan	14,300
1783	Laki, Iceland	9,350
1919	Kelut, Indonesia	5,100
1882	Galunggung, Indonesia	4,000
1631	Vesuvius, Italy	3,500
79	Vesuvius, Italy	3,350

GLOSSARY

ash Powder made up of tiny pieces of glassy rock.

ash cloud A large cloud of ash blown into the air by a volcano. Also called an eruption column.

boundary Where the edges of two tectonic plates meet.

caldera A giant hole in the ground or on the seabed formed when the ground collapses into the empty magma chamber of a volcano.

cinder cone A volcano made from a heap of cinders.

cinders Small pieces of red or black rock filled with gas bubbles.

composite cone A steep-sided volcano that is made up of layers of ash and lava.

constructive boundary A boundary where two tectonic plates move away from each other and new rock forms in the gap that is made.

crater A bowl-shaped hole in the top of a volcano.

crust The solid outer layer of the earth.

destructive boundary A boundary where two tectonic plates move toward each other and one dips into the Earth and melts.

forge The place where a blacksmith works, bending and hammering red-hot iron into objects.

glacier A slow-moving river of ice that flows down a valley in high mountain ranges.

hot-spot volcano A volcano in the middle of a tectonic plate, over a hot spot in the earth's crust (a place where magma forces its way to the surface).

lava Molten or solid rock on the surface that has come from a volcano.

magma Molten rock deep under the earth's surface.

magma chamber A magma-filled space deep under a volcano.

mudflow A fast-moving mixture of ash and water. Also called a lahar.

pyroclastic flow A thick cloud of red-hot ash and rock that flows down the side of a volcano.

seismometer A device that measures tiny vibrations in the ground.

shield volcano A low, wide volcano made of lava flows piled on top of each other.

tectonic plate One of the giant pieces that make up the earth's crust.

tuff A type of rock made from compressed layers of volcanic ash.

vent A hole through the middle of a volcano from which ash and lava escape.

FURTHER INFORMATION

Books

Farndon, John. *How The Earth Works*. Dorling Kindersley, 1992.

Ganeri, Anita. *Horrible Geography: Violent Volcanoes*. Scholastic, 1999.

Newson, Lesley. *The Atlas of the World's Worst Natural Disasters*. Dorling Kindersley, 1998.

Oxdale, Chris. *Earth's Changing Landscape: Earthquakes and Volcanoes*. Franklin Watts, 2004.

Web sites

www.visibleearth.nasa.gov
Includes a collection of images of volcanoes taken by NASA spacecraft.

www.volcanoes.com
Contains hundreds of links to volcano sites.

www.volcanoworld.org
Lots of information, photographs, and videos about volcanoes around the world.

www.swisseduc.ch/stromboli
Site dedicated to eruptions of Stromboli but also has photographs and videos of other volcanoes.

Videos/DVDs

Volcano: Nature's Inferno. (National Geographic, 2000).

Eyewitness: Volcano. (Dorling Kindersley, 2000).

INDEX

Page numbers in **bold** refer to illustrations.